X-RAY

Vision

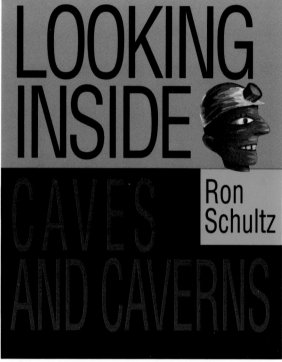

LOOKING INSIDE
CAVES AND CAVERNS

Ron Schultz

ILLUSTRATED BY
Nick Gadbois and Peter Aschwanden

John Muir Publications
Santa Fe, New Mexico

Acknowledgments

I would like to express my grateful appreciation to the following people for their willing cooperation, open phone lines, and their excellent information. Without them this book would not have been possible. Ronal Kerbo has been the inspiration and well-spring for this project. An extraordinary effort has been made by Ron to aid this project and my appreciation for that goes beyond these humble thanks. In addition, Dr. Michael Queen, Carlsbad Cave Specialist Dale Pate, and National Park Service Interpreter Vivian Satori provided valued time and explanations of this underground world. The photographs found in these pages were contributed by some wonderful, supportive people: Dave Jagnow, Diane Northup, Kenneth Ingham, John Brooks, the National Park Service, Bill Elliot, and Jerry Trout. I would also like to express my continued gratitude to the staff of John Muir Publications for their support, ideas, and a wonderful working environment.

This book is dedicated to
my parents,
who understand the value of exploring
inner worlds

John Muir Publications, P.O. Box 613, Santa Fe,
New Mexico 87504

Printed in the United States of America
Printed on recycled paper

First edition. First printing September 1993.
First TWG printing September 1993

Library of Congress Cataloging-in-Publication
Data
  Schultz, Ron, (Ronald), 1951-
   Looking inside caves and caverns /
   by Ron Schultz
     p.   cm. — (X-ray vision)
   Includes index.
   Summary: Explores the world of caves and
  describes the work of speleologists and cavers.
   ISBN 1-56261-126-7
   1. Caves—Juvenile literature.   [1.Caves]
  I. Title.   II. Series.
  GB601.2.S38   1993
  551.4'47 — dc20   93-13159
                                        CIP
                                         AC

Logo Design: Peter Aschwanden
Design: KenWilson
Illustrations: Peter Aschwanden, Nick Gadbois
Typeface: ITC Lubalin Graph
Printer: Guynes Printing Company

Distributed to the book trade by
W. W. Norton & Co.
500 Fifth Ave.
New York, New York 10110

Distributed to the education market by
The Wright Group
19201 120th Avenue N.E.
Bothell, WA 98011

Contents

Ronal Kerbo

Introduction

Way down, water drips in darkened caverns, and bats roost in jumbled clusters. Way down, beneath the world of light, is a place of awesome beauty, magnificent formations, and mind-boggling stretches of undisturbed time. This is the realm of caves. Buried in the dark are delicate rock decorations that line the walls, cling to the ceilings, and rise from the floors. There are vanilla ice-cream-like flowstones, rock sheets of rippled draperies, long dangling soda straws of stone, towering water-melted mineral columns, lacy crystals called popcorn, ceiling-dwelling stalactites, and floor-hugging stalagmites.

The majority of these cave marvels have formed over millions of years. They are found in areas around the world where the land was once underwater. Most caves are made up of limestone, a kind of rock formed from the decayed remains of underwater plants and animals. Limestone is called a sedimentary rock because it is made up of sediment, the material that settles to the bottom of bodies of water.

Many of these once-submerged limestone areas are now places where mountain ranges have been pushed up from ancient oceans.

The name scientists have given to the countryside where caves are located is **karst**. Actually, Karst is a cave-filled area in what was once Yugoslavia, in eastern Europe. **Geologists**, scientists who study how the Earth formed, now refer to all cave country throughout the world as karst.

Photo courtesy of Carlsbad Caverns

King's Palace, Carlsbad Caverns, New Mexico

Into these darkened chambers come the cavers—people of all ages who shimmy and squirm through narrow cave entrances, their pale helmet lights illuminating their rocky paths. They explore caves to map and study their formations. This is called **speleology**. (In Greek, *spelaion* means cave, and *logos* means study). **Speleologists** are scientists who study caves. It was from the word speleology that a journalist once made up the name "spelunkers" to describe those who explore caves. Today, most of these people prefer to be known simply as **cavers**. Their motto is, "Take only pictures, kill nothing but time, and leave nothing, not even footprints."

Cavers know that caves are a world of unspoiled wonder, of ageless development, and of fragile balance. It is a domain to be seen and not touched. It is a terrain to be marveled at, but never disturbed. So, enter with us now as we "cave softly" and explore the extraordinary spectacle to be found when we look inside caves and caverns.

Soda straw cave decorations

NICK GADBOIS

People who explore caves prefer to be known as "cavers," not "spelunkers"

How Caves Become Caves

he words **cave** and **cavern** actually refer to the same thing—a hollow space underground. Cavern is just a fancy name for cave. Since some of the caves we will explore have taken over a million years to form, they've had lots of time to become pretty fancy.

As we said earlier, limestone caves are formed in karst country. The mountains in this area are covered with all sizes of cracks and fissures. It is through these slits and crevices that water tumbles, drips, and pours. This water is mixed with carbon dioxide, the remains of decayed plants. When water and carbon dioxide come together, it produces **carbonic acid**. Acid is a corrosive substance that acts just like gazillions of tiny mouths, eating away whatever it comes in contact with. That's exactly what carbonic acid does to limestone. It gobbles right through these rocky deposits, slowly chomping and dissolving the limestone away until, after a couple million-year-long meals, it has eaten away an entire cave. This mixture of rock and carbonic acid is called a solution. A solution is a mixture of one or more dissolved substances. This is why limestone caves are called **solution caves**.

People used to think that caves were created by fast-moving underground rivers and streams, just like canyons and mesas. But geologists found that caves were formed by water moving much more slowly. When the land was pushed up from the ocean floor, the limestone rose above the water level, causing cracks and fractures in its surface. These cracks allowed the carbonic acid to seep down and form the cave and all its amazingly beautiful decorations.

Unlike caves in mountainous areas, some caves remain underwater. The cracks that form in them are produced by the sheer weight of all the layers of limestone on top of one another.

Limestone caves formed when the land pushed up from the ocean, causing cracks and fissues

LIMESTONE UPTHRUST

WATER TABLE

PETER ASCHWANDEN

Often, passageways are dissolved away between rocks that aren't affected by acidic water. These rocks are called insoluble, meaning they don't dissolve. When caves are first being formed, the rock-eating water moves at about the same rate into all the cracks and joints between the rocks. But as larger channels are gulped down and opened up by the acid and water, more water can move in and speed up the process.

Compared to the ancient age of the land around them, caves are youngsters. The area around Carlsbad Caverns in New Mexico is over 250 million years old, while the caves themselves are less than 10 million years old.

Carbonic acid dissolves soluble rock to create a solution formation

Cave Parts

There are three main parts to a cave: the entrance, the twilight zone, and the dark zone. Like crystals, no two cave entrances are alike. An entrance may be a large opening in the side of a mountain, an open pit, or a small crevice stuck between rocks. Many people have thoughtlessly dumped their trash into open pits, not realizing they were entrances into remarkable underground caverns. In some cases, a cave entrance might be covered with plants and trees. This growth might even extend into the entrance itself.

The entrance to a cave

The twilight zone and dark zone

The twilight zone is not a supernatural breeding ground for the weird and mysterious. It is simply that part of a cave beyond the entrance where light still penetrates. As long as you can still see, you are in the twilight zone. Being so close to the cave entrance, the temperature in this zone is not constant. But it is usually damp and cool. As we will see, it is also home to many different animals and bugs.

You'll know when you've stepped into the dark zone of a cave—you won't be able to see a thing. You'd better have your lights ready. It is the darkest of darks. In this zone there are no plants, just an occasional mold growing on the leftovers of animals and bats. As you shine your light around, you might find pools of water. The temperature of the air and water in the dark zone is the same. And the dampness, produced by water constantly dripping through the cracks and crevices from the soil above, can be felt everywhere. The dark zone is also the most beautiful part of a cave.

Speleothems form when dissolved calcite builds up, drop by drop

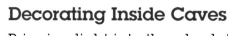
A Drop at a time

Decorating Inside Caves

Bringing light into the absolute darkness of a gigantic hollowed-out cave is a mind-shaking experience. It rattles every mental picture we have of what the world really looks like. What makes this inner-ground journey even more stupendous are the decorations that line cave walls, carpet their floors, and hang from their ceilings.

These cave-dwelling frills and fringes are called **speleothems**, basically, cave growths. Remember speleology, the study of caves? Speleothems form from water dripping from the cracks and joints in the rocks above. This water contains drops of dissolved limestone called calcite that builds up, plop by plop, to form a speleothem. Let's take a closer look at this amazing process.

Photo facing page, Ronal Kerbo

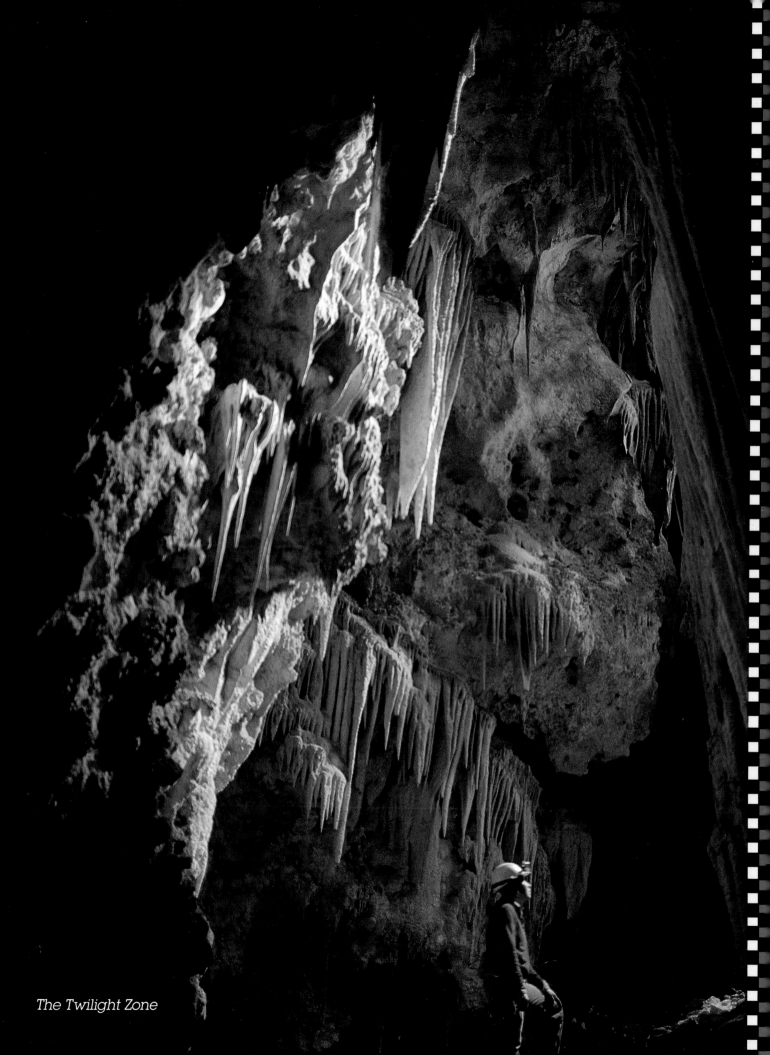

The Twilight Zone

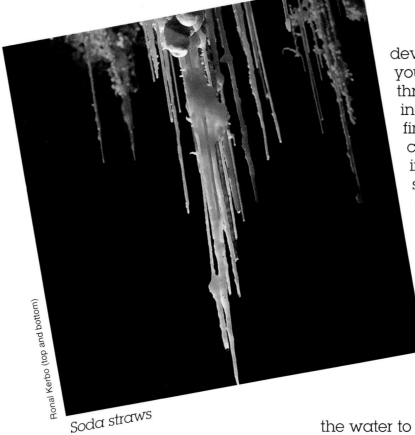

Soda straws

Remember all that rock-devouring carbonic acid? If you recall, it eats its way through the limestone leading down into a cave, and finally emerges through a crack or a joint in the ceiling. As it hangs there, it's still carrying the calcite it dissolved out of the limestone. The very first drop of water that passes through the crack in the ceiling might splat on the floor below. When it does, it leaves behind that dissolved bit of calcite. The next drop might hang on the edge of the ceiling crack long enough for the water to evaporate, leaving that pinch of calcite hanging on the lip of the crack. The next drop might do the same, extending the hanging calcite a little more, until a long decoration called a **soda straw** begins to form.

Soda straws are hollow inside. The calcite-filled acidic water flows down the inside of the straw. Because of the air in the cave, the outside of the tube dries faster than the inside. The water flows down the inside of the tube, leaving only its deposit at the end. The dulled ends of these soda straws support the hanging calcite-filled water drops until the water evaporates, depositing its mineral grain.

Eventually, calcite-filled water will run over the outside of the soda straw. Drop by drop, the calcite is left behind and forms a speleothem that dangles from the ceiling, seeming to defy gravity as it stretches toward the floor below. These are called **stalactites**. (One way to remember them is "C" for ceiling.)

The same dripping process is used to form speleothems that seem to sprout from the ground. These are called **stalagmites**. (Remember "G" for ground.) Water dropping from the ceiling leaves behind its leftover calcite lunch on the floor below. Then, one on top of the next, a new rock formation grows up from that first plop. As you might imagine, drop by drop is not a very fast process. This is one reason why cavers never touch or take anything from a cave. It just takes too long to make these incredible constructions—thousands and thousands of years, in fact!

Stalagmite and stalactite

One of the weirdest looking speleothems is the **helictite**. Unlike the stalactite and stalagmite, helictites grow in more than one direction. For years, the formation of these free spirits of the cave world baffled scientists. We know now that these curling, twisted wall-dwellers are hollow. Through that tiny canal, water is pushed from a small hole in the cave wall toward its tip. That itsy-bitsy, teeny-weeny amount of water is so small and flows so slowly it doesn't allow a water drop to form. Gravity has no effect on helictites. The water stops at the tip and leaves a single cone-shaped crystal of calcite. Because these crystal cones have different shapes, they don't fit perfectly on top of one another. Each one in turn becomes slightly tilted until, hundreds of years later, a curlyque of rock clings to the wall.

We will learn more about *all* of the exquisite and wondrous limestone cave decorations later when we journey "Into the Cave." For now, we can marvel at the unbelievable drop-by-drop development of these beautiful re-formed rocks.

David Jagnow

A maze of helictites

The Solution to Dissolving Solutions

Many of the world's most beautiful caves are solution caves, dissolved from great limestone deposits. You can see for yourself how this process works by following these steps.

1. In a bowl, mix 1 cup of salt with 2 cups of flour. Slowly add 1 cup of water, mixing and kneading the mixture until the dough forms a ball. Cut the dough into four equal pieces.

2. With your parents' help, turn the oven on to 250 degrees. Bake one of the pieces of dough for 15 to 20 minutes, until the ball is hard.

3. Gradually add small amounts of water to the second piece and stir until it becomes a smooth watery paste.

4. To the third piece, gradually add an even smaller amount of water and stir until it becomes a thick wet goo.

5. Leave the fourth piece a soft ball.

6. In a large baking pan, place the baked piece of dough and the soft ball piece on either side of the pan. Slowly drip water on each piece from above. What happens to the pieces of dough and the watery solutions they create? Does one dissolve faster or more evenly? This gives you an idea of how acidic water dissolves limestone into caves.

7. Next, place a small drinking glass upside down in the pan and slowly pour a little of the watery paste portion down the sides. When that dries, apply a second and third coat. You've created flowstones.

8. Finally, pick up the thick wet goo and hold it over the pan. Allow the goo to drip off your fingers. As it drips, look at the forms it makes. What cave formation does it look like? Now look at the forms the goo makes as it falls into the pan, dropping one bit on top of the other. You've created a stalagmite.

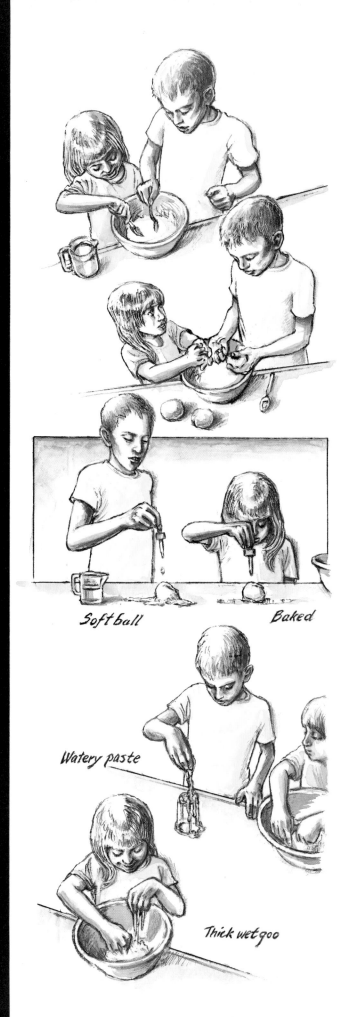

Soft ball

Baked

Watery paste

Thick wet goo

Alive in the Cave

Shelter from the Storm

They crawl, they flip, they fly, they swim, they hop, they scurry, they even sleep upside down, and sometimes they growl. From bats to beetles, from ringtail cats to blind fish, they are the cave critters. Caves spread their life forms from entrance to darkest cranny. Thousands of years ago, even humans lived in caves. They stayed very close to the entrance, rarely venturing beyond the edge of the twilight zone. Today, caves are inhabited only by smaller creatures.

In the summer months, cave swallows dart in and out of the cave entrance, building nests among the warm rocks and in the cracks and corners of the twilight zone. Within the entrance and twilight zones, green plants may grow. Snakes, frogs, and slimy salamanders also hop and slither around the rocks surrounding a cave's opening. On occasion, ringtail cats or raccoons find their way into the cave, searching for food. Pack rats hide in the rock folds, building their grassy nests, and scurry out at night. Owls, on their nightly dinner raids, swoop into the cave entrance after small rodents. In some caves with vertical entrances, people have found the remains of dogs, cats, cows, goats, and horses.

In the twilight zone cave pools, cavers will find brown crayfish, eyed flatworms, frogs, eyed amphipods that look like tiny shrimp, snails, and tiny cave fish. Further into the dark zone of the cave are similar life forms. The only difference is that the dark zone water-dwellers are usually white and blind. When you live in total darkness, eyes are of little use.

Salamander

Crayfish

Blind catfish

David Jagnow

William R. Elliott

Diane Northrup/Kenneth Ingham

Cave Paintings

Thousands and thousands of years ago, early humans lived in caves in what we now call Europe. Anthropologists named these people Cro-Magnons. Unlike earlier races, Cro-Magnons created beautiful paintings on the walls and ceilings of their caves, the only artist's canvas they knew. They painted the animals around them as they saw them, as well as scenes from daily life, such as hunting and childbirth. They etched and scratched their drawings, then filled them in with paint. They made red, brown, and yellow paints from the minerals and plants they found nearby, and black from charcoal. Explorers have discovered a number of these exquisite cave painting sites in Spain and France. In many other areas of the world as well, we find the creative expression and record of daily life these cave dwellers left behind.

You too can make your own "cave paintings" and see how difficult it is to draw on a bumpy surface. Take a brown supermarket shopping bag and cut it with scissors down one side. Then cut out the bottom section so you have a long piece of brown paper. Crumple the paper, and then smooth it out as best you can. Then use red, brown, black, and yellow crayons, markers, or paints to draw your own "cave paintings."

Creatures that live their whole lives within caves without ever leaving are called **troglodytes**. Those that can live in or out of the cave environment, but prefer the cave, are called **troglophiles**, or cave lovers. Cavers might be considered a mutant form of troglophile, although they more closely resemble **trogloxenes** who, like bats, must occasionally return to the surface and exit the cave.

During the winter, larger animals seek shelter in the cave from the harsh cold, normally staying in the entrance area. By this time of the year, all the cave-dwelling birds have headed south for warmer climates.

Moving into the winter twilight zone, the ceilings of the cave become covered with huddled harvestmen (also known as daddy longlegs), spider-like creatures. Keeping the harvestmen company on their lofty perch are the moths and the cave crickets. During the summer months, these creepy crawlies do their thing outside the cave.

Diane Northrup/Kenneth Ingham

Cave spider (above) and cave cricket (below)

Vampire bat

On the Wing

Further into the cave, clinging to the walls and ceilings, are the bats. Big brown bats, Mexican free-tail bats, long-eared bats, lump-nosed bats, gray bats, social bats, vampire bats (none in the U.S.), pygmy bats—at last count within Carlsbad Caverns in New Mexico, researchers had found over a dozen different kinds of bats. Each prefers its own different climate zone in the cave. Carlsbad is home to over a million bats, most of them Mexican free-tails. During the summer months, they put on a spectacular aerial display as they leave the cave together at sunset. Some bats fly fifty miles in a single night in search of food before returning to their roost.

Bats are also a source of food for many creatures living in the dark parts of a cave. Feeding on the guano (the solid waste of bats) are beetles and their larvae, flatworms, and even cave spiders. Bat guano is also an excellent fertilizer. In fact, the orange groves that used to thrive throughout southern California were fed on guano extracted from Carlsbad Caverns.

Inside the dark zone, a caver may come across white crickets, blind fish, crayfish, blind salamanders, mites (tiny spider-like critters), and in some tropical caves, even massive cockroaches. The shrimp-like crayfish and the fish are all leftovers from ancient times when the caves were under water.

In most North American caves, once a caver has passed through the cave entrance zone, there are very few, if any, crawly critters that can do a human any harm. However, in the more tropical caves of Mexico, Central, and South America, it's best to be well aware of the more dangerous insect dwellers of the deep. Cavers are always prepared: they are often traveling in territory never seen by another living human.

Bats making their exit through the natural entrance to Carlsbad Caverns at dusk

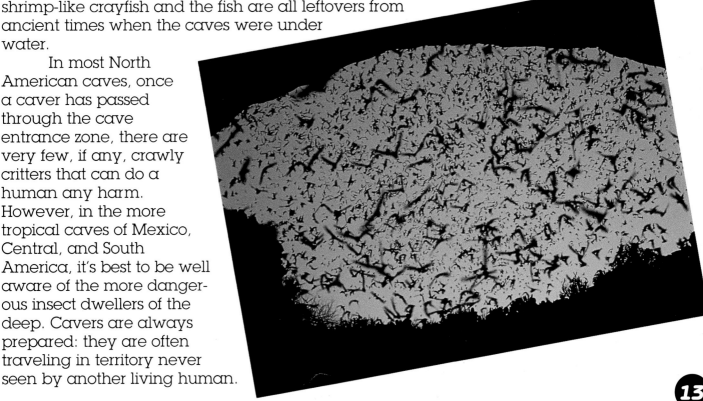

Caving Tools

Many caves throughout the world have been commercially developed for people of all ages to enjoy. To see these caves requires nothing more than a good pair of shoes and strong legs. The majority of caves, however, are not developed. These are called "wild" caves. For a caver to explore a wild cave requires a few more tools besides shoes.

Caves are formed in two basic directions, up and down (vertical) and side to side (horizontal). Before we start traveling up and down walls like that famous bat-like cape crusader, let's take a look at the equipment necessary to explore caves that follow a more horizontal path.

Lighting the Way

Once we enter the dark zone, the first piece of equipment we need becomes immediately obvious: a light. Cavers carry a minimum of three different sources of light. One of these sources should be attached to a helmet, another mandatory piece of equipment. When caving, a helmet is *not* optional. There are two basic kinds of helmet lights: electric, which run on batteries, and carbide lamps, which use a flame. Carbide is a chemical that combines with water to produce a gas. This gas comes out of a small tube in the lamp. When ignited, it produces a flame whose glare bounces off a reflector.

Both of these light sources have their advantages and disadvantages. Batteries for electric lights are heavy, and the light they produce is not as bright or wide as that from a carbide lamp. Electric lights are easier to operate, but carbide lamps are lighter. On long cave trips, the less weight a caver carries the

Caving tools: three light sources, boots, and gloves

Jerry Trout

One small problem with carbide lamps

better. There is another reason some cavers prefer carbide over electric light: the flame. Cavers have actually been saved by the combined warmth of the flame and a special outdoor blanket called a space blanket. Of course, there have also been many instances of carbide flames burning the bottoms of the cavers crawling in front of them or catching a companion's hair on fire! Care needs to be taken.

Cavers who use carbide lamps also carry a small repair kit, filled with all the replaceable parts of the lamp. Electric lamp users need to carry spare bulbs and batteries. The other two light sources a caver totes are usually of the small flashlight variety. The last thing a caver wants is to be three miles back in a cave and have all the lights go out. Retracing a dangerous route through unseen stalagmites and over treacherous rock falls is a sure way to ruin more than a day.

Dressing the Part

What does the well-dressed caver wear? Certainly nothing you'd wear to the mall—unless of course that mall was filled with jagged, water-bathed rock formations, barely body-width passageways, and prehistoric dust.

Cave fashion begins with the underclothes. Polyprophaline is the latest man-made fabric to keep a body warm and dry. It's the same material used for under-ski apparel.

Over this base, a caver dons rugged outer clothes. These clothes have to be able to take some pretty heavy abuse. Corduranylon, the same stuff they make nylon ropes and packs from, is super-tough and can withstand the tear and torture of clawing rocks. T-shirts and jeans, and in some cases shorts, are all right for warm weather caves as long as the caver is wearing knee and elbow pads.

Resembling an underground skateboarder, a caver isn't concerned about looking cool. These soft-padded body covers allow the caver to get as much surface of the body as possible on the rock—without pain. Climbing up and over sharp-edged crevices, a person wants every bit of knee, elbow, toe, and bottom on rock to keep from falling.

White-soled, ankle-high hiking boots are also standard equipment. They should be white-soled because the color in black soles comes off on the cave trail. Remember: a caver leaves nothing behind, not even footprints.

For cavers who want to delve into the frozen world of ice caves, appropriate outerwear is essential. Parkas, socks, and proper footwear are required in these frigid inner reaches.

To protect against dehydration, cavers carry a canteen filled with water. After any physical exertion, it's important to refresh the body. In addition to water, cavers need to carry food: high-energy bars, peanuts, or chocolate are all excellent sources of fast energy. If the trip is for longer than a day, a small camp stove will have to be packed in, along with some of that *delicious* freeze-dried food-like substance (if you're hungry, anything tastes good!). Everything gets carried out when a caver leaves—wrappers, food scraps, everything. Small camp stoves that carry their own fuel can be used for heating water,

Remember, if you pack it in, pack it out

but starting a camp fire in a cave is not acceptable. The smoke and soot would cover the decorations, ruining them for others.

To complete their tool kit for entering horizontal caves, cavers carry a rugged, heavy canvas or cordura-nylon back pack. It's got to be rugged—it will be dragged through crawlways, lowered on ropes, and squished through cracks and crevices. And it's got to be flexible—these packs are worn in various ways: on the back, attached to the ankle to be dragged through crawlways, or like a fanny pack.

Jerry Trout

Caving gear

The Vertical Approach

When a cave has a ledge with a drop-off of more than 10 feet, a caver needs some traveler's aids—also called ropes. The nylon ropes made today are stronger, more durable, and longer than ever before. Like the clothes on a caver's back, these ropes have to be tough. The last thing a caver wants is to be hanging in midair 200 feet above the cave floor—and have the sharp rocks above slice through her rope.

The correct word for roping down is **abseiling**. However, just as in rock climbing, cavers use the word **rappel**, which in French actually means "to retrieve." But then, what goes down also has to come back up.

There are a number of rapelling devices to aid a caver on the trip down. A seat harness allows the descending caver to slowly lower herself to the bottom. Gloves are essential to prevent rope burn from the friction as the rope slides through the hands. The rope is looped through the seat harness and the rappel rack, which controls the speed of the sliding rope. Attaching the caver to all of this are snap clips called **carabineers**, or "biners" for short.

A caver rappeling out of a cave

Vertical caving gear

17

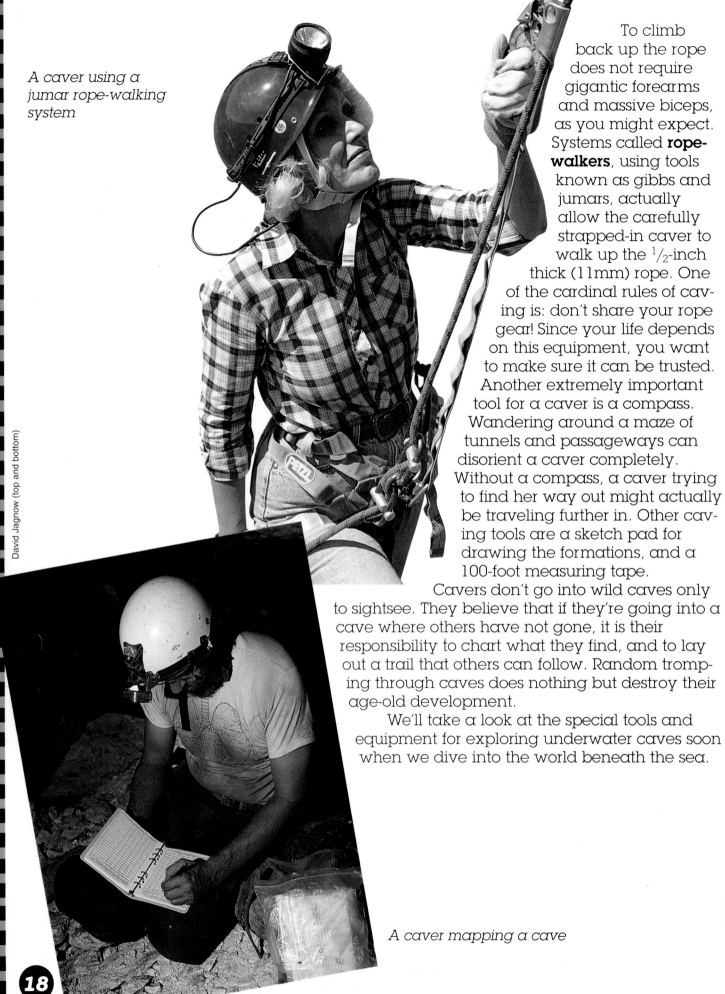

A caver using a jumar rope-walking system

To climb back up the rope does not require gigantic forearms and massive biceps, as you might expect. Systems called **rope-walkers**, using tools known as gibbs and jumars, actually allow the carefully strapped-in caver to walk up the ½-inch thick (11mm) rope. One of the cardinal rules of caving is: don't share your rope gear! Since your life depends on this equipment, you want to make sure it can be trusted. Another extremely important tool for a caver is a compass. Wandering around a maze of tunnels and passageways can disorient a caver completely. Without a compass, a caver trying to find her way out might actually be traveling further in. Other caving tools are a sketch pad for drawing the formations, and a 100-foot measuring tape.

Cavers don't go into wild caves only to sightsee. They believe that if they're going into a cave where others have not gone, it is their responsibility to chart what they find, and to lay out a trail that others can follow. Random tromping through caves does nothing but destroy their age-old development.

We'll take a look at the special tools and equipment for exploring underwater caves soon when we dive into the world beneath the sea.

A caver mapping a cave

Caver descending into Lechugilla Cave, New Mexico

Into the Cave

Donning our cave gear, it is time to enter the world of caves. There are five different kinds of caves we will journey into: limestone, gypsum, underwater, and glacier caves, and lava tubes. So let's turn on our cave lights and crawl on in.

Limestone Caves

Drip by drip, drop by drop, year by year, magnificent water-melted rock formations are etched and deposited onto the ceilings, floors, and walls of limestone caves. Few things on earth are as awe-inspiring as a speleothem-decorated room in a cave. And even fewer are as beautiful as the Big Room at Carlsbad Caverns.

Hall of Giants in Carlsbad Caverns

Discovering the Wonders of Carlsbad Caverns

It was over a thousand years ago that Native Americans used the entrance and twilight zone of Carlsbad Cavern for shelter. In the 1800s, settlers in southern New Mexico were drawn to the cave's natural entrance by the summer evening bat swarms. As enterprising westerners, many of them began mining the vast supply of bat guano as fertilizer.

A cowboy named Jim White was one of those early miners. But White was interested in more than just bat guano—the lure of the dark called him. With crude kerosene lanterns, White began exploring the inner parts of the cave in the early 1900s. Without the benefit of modern climbing equipment, White rigged a bat guano bucket to lower himself 170 feet down into the cave. When he returned from his first trip with tales of a pristine underworld filled with fantastic cave formations, people didn't believe him.

In 1915, photographs taken by Ray V. Davis proved to disbelievers that White was telling the truth. Eight years later, after the National Geographic Society explored Carlsbad, the U.S. Department of Interior proclaimed it a national monument. Since then, millions of people have marveled at Carlsbad Cavern, one of the world's great limestone caves.

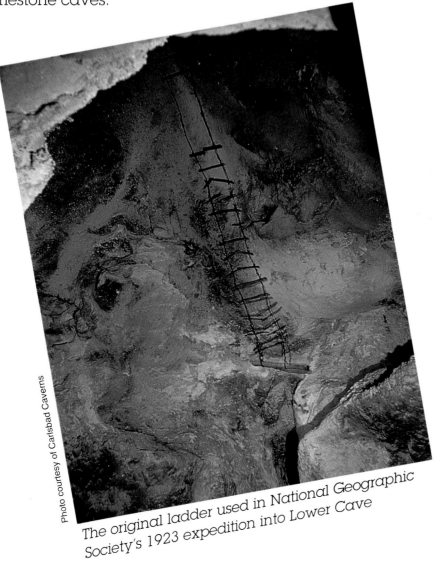

Photo courtesy of Carlsbad Caverns

The original ladder used in National Geographic Society's 1923 expedition into Lower Cave

Jim White descended into Carlsbad Cavern in a guano bucket

The Capitan Reef in New Mexico and Texas

The Birth of Carlsbad

What these visitors have found are extraordinary rooms filled with stalagmites and stalactites. It wasn't always this way. Carlsbad was once part of a giant reef ringing an inland sea. The reef formed over 250 million years ago, during what is known as the Permian era. This was a time when the earth was dramatically growing and changing. Over many thousands of years, forces from within the earth pushed this reef up from the bottom of the sea to become the range of mountains known today as the Guadalupe Mountains. Called the Capitan Reef, the entire reef is close to 400 miles around. It is one gigantic lump of limestone, and Carlsbad Caverns are a part of it.

Today, the area surrounding the Guadalupe Mountains is desert. Millions of years ago things were very different. The land was heavily forested. This combination of vegetation and limestone reef, covered with lots of cracks and fractures from the great upheaval, was the ideal place for caves to form.

A Speleothem Paradise

Carlsbad's main entrance path leads down a steep and winding course through wondrous expanses with names like Green Lake Room, King's Palace, and the Queen's Chamber. These rooms feature formations called **flowstones**, where calcite-filled water streamed over rocks for ages, leaving trails of deposit that look like white icing. The Doll's House is a small chamber completely filled with narrow **soda straws**, thin hollow tubes of dissolved and re-formed limestone.

Stretching down from the sides of the walls are rippled **draperies**. Looking like a rock version of the drapes you might have in your living room, these formed when beads of water trickled down a slightly slanted surface. The irregular path of the beads slowly laid down a sheet of calcite. Draperies are beautiful formations, especially when they are illuminated from behind, and their translucent, almost see-through, quality is highlighted.

Scattered throughout Carlsbad are cool, clear pools of water. Unfortunately, some unthinking tourists drop coins into these pools, which pollutes them. Holding some of these pools back are tiny ledges called **rimstone dams**. Many rimstone dams are formed like terraces, one above the next, and encircle water only a few inches deep. Others form pools large enough to swim through. These rimstone dams were created when calcite was deposited as water flowed over the tops of the dam.

David Jagnow

Lake of the Clouds, Carlsbad Caverns

Photo facing page, Ronal Kerbo

The Klansman, Carlsbad Caverns

*Popcorn, also called
cave coral*

Aragonite

Into the Big Room

Descending deeper into Carlsbad, 750 feet to the floor of the Big Room, curlyque helictites reach out from the sides of the wall. These slow-forming cave mysteries were twisted and bent in part by the air current that flows through a cave. One of the world's leading speleologists, Dr. Michael Queen, discovered that as the hot, moist air in a cave rises from the floor, cooler air is pushed down the cave walls. This gently flowing air slowly redirects and bends helictites while they form.

This air flow also causes a bumpy-lumpy decoration called **popcorn** to develop on stalagmites and cave walls. It is also known as **cave coral** because it looks similar to the coral found in the sea. The moisture in the cave, caught in the rising and falling air, contains tiny bits of calcite dissolved inside. When the airborne moisture condenses onto the rocks, just like the moisture from your breath condenses on a window pane, it creates a knobby formation that looks like a popped kernel of corn.

Aragonite is another form of the calcium carbonate mineral that calcite comes from. It creates some of the most beautiful spiky crystal formations found in caves. Aragonite helictites look like clear-needled sea urchins. Unlike its calcite relative, aragonite prefers warmer caves and is not found in colder northern areas.

Similar to aragonite helictites are **gypsum needles**. Like calcite, **gypsum** is a mineral, the product of sulfuric acid combined with limestone. Gypsum needles are slender, glassy gypsum threads that grow out of the sediments on the cave floor. Unlike helictites, gypsum needles grow from the base of the needle, rather than from the tip. The formation known as the **gypsum flower** also grows in the same fashion. Like toothpaste being squeezed from a tube, the gypsum flower's curling petals actually push out from cave walls.

The massive gypsum deposits in the Carlsbad area were created millions of years ago. Natural sulfuric acid welled up from underneath the reef. When it combined with limestone and the water within evaporated, it formed gypsum. Gypsum is dissolved much more easily by water than calcite is, and is often washed out of the cave during the cave's formation. This explains why there is so little gypsum left in Carlsbad. In a little while, we'll look inside some caves made almost entirely out of gypsum.

In addition to stalactites and stalagmites, some rooms feature massive **columns** that stretch from floor to ceiling. These columns of re-formed rock are produced when a stalactite from above meets a stalagmite from below. There are a number of these at Carlsbad. One used to be called "The Eternal Kiss," until speleologists looked more closely. They discovered there was actually a tissue-thin space separating the two tips.

Photo courtesy of Carlsbad Caverns

The Eternal Kiss

Lechugilla Cave, New Mexico

Exploring the Unexplored

The total length of passageways throughout Carlsbad Caverns is about 26 miles. Mammoth Cave in Kentucky, the world's longest cave, is 330 miles long. Carlsbad's Big Room is the seventh largest cave room in the world in floor space. This cave, however, is only one of 80 caves known to exist in Carlsbad Caverns National Park. In 1986, just 4 $\frac{1}{2}$ miles from Carlsbad, cavers discovered new passages in Lechuguilla Cave. Today, more than 60 miles of passageways have already been charted here, and those miles have quickly revealed to cavers that Lechuguilla is one of the world's greatest caves.

Not only are the decorations in Lechuguilla Cave of unsurpassed beauty, but cavers have found formations they have never seen before. Helictites, only seen before in dry caves, were found here growing underwater. The marvels of Lechuguilla are still unfolding. To descend into this cave requires a 90-foot rappel, followed by a 150-foot rappel. The cave itself is about 1,600 feet deep, about $\frac{1}{4}$-mile down.

The floor of Carlsbad's Big Room is about 750 feet beneath the surface, and there is still a great deal of unexplored territory in this cave, too. More than 200 feet above the floor is a large opening covered with stalagmites. This was obviously a main channel for water into the room. In order to explore that chamber, Ronal Kerbo, once Carlsbad's cave specialist and now National Park Service's Cave Management Specialist, tied a rope to a helium balloon and floated it up to the opening. Guiding the rope, Kerbo hooked it around a stalagmite in the opening. Then, by attaching a climbing rope to the first rope, he was able to climb up and over the floor of the cavern. In doing so, Kerbo discovered a beautiful passage leading back to a large room he named Spirit World.

For Kerbo and many of his associates, caves represent one of the last places on earth where no human has ever been before. People may not have climbed to the top of every mountain or surveyed every jungle, but they have flown over them, photographed them, and mapped them. Wild caves and wild parts of developed caves have never even been seen before. The thrill of exploration is what drives people like Ron Kerbo to climb a rope 200 feet above the floor of a cave, risking life and limb. As Kerbo says, "What better to risk everything on, than adventure?" The discovery of a beautiful chamber, however, is his real reward.

Photo facing page, David Jagnow

Ronal Kerbo used a helium ballon to position his ropes in Carlsbad's Big Room

27

Going Off-Trail

Donning a caver's helmet and light, my guide and I descended a metal ladder into Carlsbad's Lower Cave. This is one of the five areas of Carlsbad Caverns that is not developed. The feeling of descending into total darkness was awesome. Wherever we looked, our headlights suddenly illuminated the unseen. Shadowy scenes of popcorn-covered stalagmites and stalactites stretched before us. We walked gently on the rocky path. The only sounds were our feet on the path and the occasional dripping of water. Draperies and flowstones cascaded down the walls around us. We squeezed through narrow openings and crawled beneath rock overhangs barely big enough for our bodies. There was no one else in this cave but us.

As we wandered through this wild section of Carlsbad, we saw a pocket of cave pearls. Similar to the pearls created in oysters, these small, smooth, round calcite deposits formed by a slow and continual turning process. Water, passing over the small crater in which they lie, gently rotates the pearls for hundreds of years. People used to take cave pearls as mementos of their trips to Carlsbad. Now, Carlsbad receives packages returning cave pearls from visitors who regret their earlier thoughtlessness.

The author descending into Carlsbad's Lower Cave

Laura Sanderford

In the middle of this off-trail trip, we found a quiet place and turned off our lights. We could see absolutely nothing, not even our hands held in front of our eyes. Standing in total darkness and silence, except for a drip of water here and there, was one of the most spiritual experiences I have ever had. Secure that nothing was lurking in the dark, we felt completely at ease. Our inner thoughts were all we could hear. There are many reasons for exploring caves. This journey into one of the world's foremost limestone caves taught us a great deal about caves and about ourselves.

Cave pearls form in small craters

David Jagnow (top and bottom)

Gypsum Caves

Gypsum caves are created the same way their limestone cousins are: water seeps through cracks and fractures and dissolves the rock. And, like limestone caves, gypsum caves are solution caves, dissolved from limestone. But the main difference between limestone and gypsum caves is that limestone caves are made of limestone and calcite, the mineral formed when carbonic acid combines with limestone. Gypsum caves are made from limestone and gypsum, the mineral formed when sulfuric acid combines with limestone and the liquid evaporates.

Inside, gypsum caves look very similar to limestone-calcite caves. Because gypsum dissolves more easily than limestone, any water flowing through a gypsum cave prevents large decorations like stalagmites or stalactites from forming. This is true even though small gypsum speleothems form faster than those made of calcite. Depending on the amount of water in a cave, gypsum flowers and helictites can often be found on the walls, along with other small cave decorations. The sparkling, icing-white color of these gypsum decorations makes them especially beautiful.

Gypsum caves normally have oval passageways that follow distinct patterns as they proceed down. In fact, trained speleologists can tell how deep they are in a gypsum cave by the changes in the shape of the passageway. In the entrance area, the oval passage is wider than it is high because the gypsum is embedded with rocks that don't dissolve. Inside the cave, in the area where the fractures and cracks above drip water directly into the gypsum, the cave becomes much higher than it is wide. This is because there are no rocks to restrict the dissolution (dissolving) of the gypsum.

The Crystal Chandelier, massive gypsum flowers in Lechuguilla Cave, New Mexico

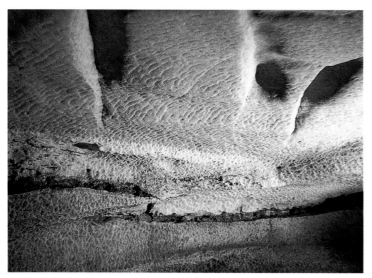

Gypsum cave

29

Underwater Caves

The earth is a living planet and its land forms are constantly changing. As recently as 100,000 years ago, most of North America and Europe were covered by a great sheet of ice. At that time, many of the caves in places like Florida, Mexico, and the Bahamas were actually above water. But as the ice began to melt about 40,000 years ago, the waters in the oceans began to rise. From about 20,000 years ago to about 5,000 years ago, the waters in the Atlantic and Caribbean rose between 100 and 300 feet. In doing so, they flooded the caves in areas that had once been dry.

Two main reasons have convinced scientists that most underwater caves were once dry caves. First, they have found cave decorations that could only have formed in dry caves. Second, they have discovered Indian remains, revealing that the caves were once used as dry burial sites, and most likely for shelter, too.

Some underwater caves in Florida and Mexico, however, have been filled with water since the time they were formed. They do not contain the decorations that the caves pictured on these pages do. The cracks and fractures in the limestone rock were caused not by the land lifting up, as in many dry caves, but by the weight of all the layers of limestone on top of each other.

Underwater caves also feature some remarkable animal life. These include feather duster tube worms, blind cave shrimp, and blind cave fish, whose eyes have been covered by a membrane of skin. An underwater cave scientist named Jill Yager discovered another cave creature, a direct link from ancient crustaceans to the modern-day shrimp. (Crustaceans are sea creatures with hard shells and segmented bodies, such as lobsters, crabs, and shrimps.) This newly found cave creature is called a *remipedia*, which means "many-legged." It has also been nicknamed "cave swimmer." This animal is related to a creature that lived 150 million years ago. Now, *that's* a species from a lost world!

John D. Brooks

A tube worm

A remipedia, also called a cave swimmer

Photo facing page, John D. Brooks

Divers explore Saggitarius Cave in the Bahamas

Diving Down

Most underwater caves lie about 15 to 400 feet beneath the surface. Some cave divers have descended into caves close to 300 feet deep. The only way to see these underwater caves is to don scuba gear. **Scuba** stands for "self-contained underwater breathing apparatus." It was developed by the great underwater explorer Jacques Cousteau and his associate, Emil Gagnan. Scuba gear allows divers to breathe underwater without being tied to an air line above the surface. This requires tanks of compressed air. Compressed air is air whose molecules have been squished tightly together, removing all the space between them. The compressed air is then re-expanded into breathable air by devices that adjust the air flow from the tanks. These devices are called **regulators**.

Cave diving is the most dangerous form of underwater diving there is. Many people who try to cave dive never return from the experience because they weren't properly trained to handle what they encountered. The first hazard of cave diving is that a diver can't simply surface if something goes wrong—the ceiling of the cave is in the way! Second, if a diver accidently kicks up the powdery silt lying on the bottom of the cave, the rapid clouding can make it impossible to see. A diver can become completely turned around, unable to tell the ceiling from the floor or to locate the entrance—which is also the exit. A diver has only a limited amount of air in his tank. If he's 20 minutes into the cave, and it takes him 40 minutes to find his way out of a silt-filled room, and he's only carrying 60 minutes of air, he's in the kind of trouble you don't escape from.

A diver exploring Lucayan Caverns, off Grand Bahamas Island

John D. Brooks

To make sure they don't lose their way in these caves, divers attach a nylon string to the front of the cave and let it out as they swim in, very much like Hansel and Gretel's bread crumb trail. Remember, underwater caves are just as dark as dry caves. If a light should fail in an underwater cave—one of the main reasons unprepared divers drown in them—the guideline can lead the diver to safety.

A cave diver in deep trouble

To venture safely into these amazingly gorgeous caverns requires a lot of special training. It also requires that a diver carry two or more of all necessary equipment: two tanks, two regulators, five lights, and two nylon guidelines on reels. It is not uncommon for a cave diver to carry over 100 pounds of equipment.

But when all the requirements for cave diving are met, the experience is like being transported to an alien world. The Lucayan Caverns off Grand Bahamas Island have more than 7 miles of charted caves and passageways. In a cave like that, a dive can last anywhere from one to several hours. The longest known cave dive lasted over 12 hours.

Sinkholes, Cenotes, and Blue Holes

Directly connected to these underwater caves are **sinkholes** or cenotes. These formations occur on karst land that is also part of a natural aquifer. An **aquifer** is a natural underground reservoir of water. If the level in the aquifer drops, the roof of the cave suddenly has no support and the land above will sometimes collapse and sink into the cave. The cave is then jug-shaped—very narrow at the top, with a wide area underneath. Whole houses have collapsed into these sinkholes in Florida.

The land of the Yucatán Peninsula in Mexico is very similar to the land in Florida. Sinkholes in Mexico are called **cenotes**. The water beneath these cenotes is often very clear and very blue. They are very inviting to swimmers and divers. However, extreme caution is required in exploring sinkholes. They are new openings into caves, and all the dangers of cave diving apply.

Ronal Kerbo

Devil's sinkhole

33

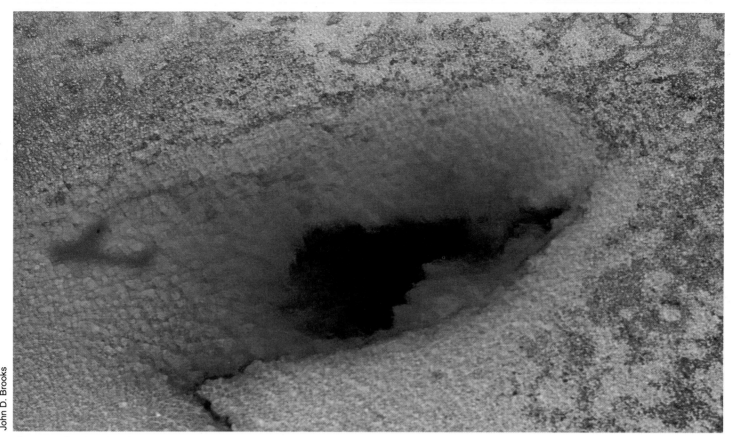

An underwater blue hole, the Bahamas

Blue holes are similar to sinkholes, but some are created by a different set of natural occurrences. Normally, blue holes appear in and around islands, and they form both in water and on land. Many blue holes form just like solution caves, during a time when the water level has dropped. But some are created when freshwater combines with saltwater that has already completely soaked a limestone bed. Where these two waters mix, carbonic acid is formed and the limestone is dissolved. Over thousands of years, passages and caves are formed.

Because the saltwater levels of the oceans rose and fell with the coming and going of the ice age, these blue holes produced caves on many different levels beneath islands. They created whole networks of caves, sometimes making the land beneath these islands look like Swiss cheese.

The formation of blue holes in freshwater and saltwater

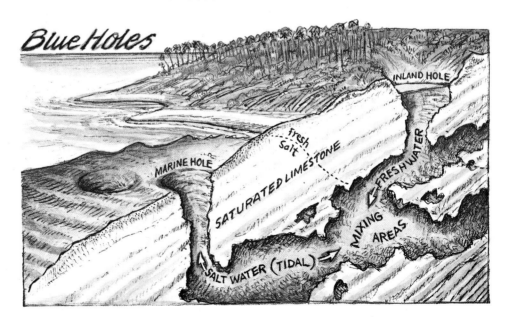

Blue Holes

INLAND HOLE

fresh
salt

MARINE HOLE

SATURATED LIMESTONE

FRESHWATER

MIXING AREAS

SALT WATER (TIDAL)

Often, the same kinds of animal life found in underwater caves are found in the saltwater parts of blue holes. Within the first 200 feet of a blue hole, divers can find sharks, moray eels, lobsters, and lots of fish. Further down in the darkness are blind fish, tube worms, and shrimps and their relatives. There are also corals, sponges, and anemones. These animals feed twice a day when the tide changes, and water rushes back and forth across their food-gathering tentacles.

Another curious event takes place around blue holes when the tides change and water rushes into them. Whirlpools are created that are strong enough to pull swimmers down into them. This daily event has spawned many island legends about a dangerous sea creature the islanders call Lusca. Half-octopus and half-shark, Lusca is said to inhabit the blue holes. When he breathes in, he creates a whirlpool and swallows any unsuspecting fisherman fishing above. "Beware de Lusca," the islanders say. "That Lusca, he bad, mahn!"

The legendary Lusca

Entrance to a lava tube, Azores Islands

Lava Tubes

A volcano violently quakes the earth, spewing forth steaming streams of molten lava. This melted rock, from deep within the earth's crust, spills down the sides of the volcano in a ribbon of fiery ooze.

Exposed to the outside air, the outer layer of the lava flow is cooled, forming a crusty, rocky exterior. Hidden within is the still blazing and gushing rock. When the eruption ends, and the blistering lava completes its run through the rock tunnel, we are left with a **lava tube**. These cave-tubes range in size from rooms with 70- to 80-foot-high ceilings to tiny cylinders barely wide enough to tummy-crawl through.

Like the rivers of lava from which they are formed, lava tubes snake down hills, curving this way and that. Sometimes they form a maze of tunnels that branch off in many directions. It's also common for one tube to form on top of another. This happens when molten lava from a volcanic eruption flows over a lava tube formed from an earlier flow. Since the roofs of these tubes are fairly thin, it's not uncommon for the wall separating the two tubes to collapse in various places. In fact, it's usually through such a roof collapse that a caver gains access to a lava tube.

Decorating with Lava

These fast-forming caves are filled with a variety of decorations. There are **lava-cicles**, which hang like icicles from the ceiling. These are produced as the lava oozes down inside the tube and the molten rock left on the ceiling drips down, like wax down a candle. Decorations that look just like stalactites and soda straws also form as the cooling lava drips off the ceiling. Like mini-waterfalls, **lava falls** measuring more than 30 feet long can also be found streaking down the wall of a lava tube.

Air flowing through these lava tubes forms a variety of other decorations from the cooling remains of molten lava. These might be twisted lava helictites, or jagged stalagmites sitting on shelves, or splatters of material on the floor that look like puddles of chocolate. In the Azores, volcanic islands off the coast of Portugal, lava tubes formed decorations of pure white silica, the material from which glass is made. Jutting from the coal black walls are spectacular glass speleothems that look like draperies, flowstones, stalactites, and stalagmites. Opals, iridescent gems, have also been known to form in lava tubes.

Because lava tubes do not hold heat well, they can get very cold—and tend to stay cold. When water pours in through cracks in the surface, it freezes, forming magnificent ice stalactites, frosty ice-falls, and beautiful, translucent ice columns.

Lava tubes are indeed wondrous and beautiful, but care should be taken in exploring them. The cooled lava rock is very sharp and jagged, and will easily tear clothes and inadequate shoes to shreds. Since little light is reflected from the coal black walls of lava tubes, cavers need especially bright lights. And, of course, a caver should never enter a lava tube in an area where a volcano is still active. That's a sure way of ending up an ex-caver and an unhappy tube decoration.

Lava tubes in the United States are found primarily in Hawaii and the western states, with excellent examples in Washington State, California, and New Mexico.

Silica speleothems in a lava tube, Azores Islands

Glacier Caves

On icy mountain tops, glaciers—rivers of ice—slowly creep downward. The weight and movement of these huge beds of ice cracks the ice. Through these fractures comes sun-warmed meltwater, melting deeper layers in the ice and causing larger cracks. Passageways have been found in glaciers measuring 10 feet high and over 20 feet wide. Rooms have been discovered that measure 250 feet long, 90 feet wide, and 25 feet high.

Inside these milky-white caverns are walls carved by incoming water. Ice blue decorations—stalagmites and stalactites, ice columns and flowstones—adorn the cave. To explore these frigid cavities takes some special preparation and equipment. Glacier cavers need especially warm clothes, mountaineering boots and equipment, and a knowledge of glacier climbing techniques. They also have to protect themselves against overexposure to cold and to watch out for massive pieces of ice that can fall from the cave ceilings without warning.

There are also a number of seasonal factors to consider when visiting glacier caves. The meltwater flow in summer is greater than at other times and can flood or make the caves a slushy mess. So glacier caves should normally only be entered during the colder months. However, to get to glacier caves usually requires climbing a mountain—and that means battling mountain weather, such as snow, fog, and winter storms. The largest ice caves in the United States are under the Paradise-Stevens Glacier on Mt. Rainier, in Washington State. Several miles of tunnels have been un-iced. Unfortunately, since glaciers are moving bodies of ice, glacier caves are not as long-lasting as their limestone relatives.

Ice cavers bundle up

Photo facing page, Ronal Kerbo

Green Lake Room, Carlsbad Caverns

Preserving Our Cave Resources

Caving Softly

"Caving softly" has two meanings: leaving caves exactly as you find them, and protecting caves because they are a valuable link to our drinking water. Caves are remarkably beautiful natural settings. They have taken millions of years to become what they are. But it doesn't take much time for one thoughtless person to break off the tip of a dangling stalactite as a souvenir—a "souvenir" that took 40,000 years to form. In Carlsbad Caverns alone, during one recent 13-year period, rangers counted over 18,000 formations broken by visitors.

Photo courtesy of Carlsbad Caverns

Broken formations, King's Palace

Caves can also be harmed by little things people don't even think about, such as lint. Like the little bits of fluff that collect in your pockets, lint falls from people's clothing as they walk through the caves and is caught by the formations. Some developed caves are visited by millions of visitors a year—and that's a lot of lint to clean up.

Cave pools have also been thoughtlessly destroyed. Tossing coins into man-made fountains may be fine, but it only pollutes nature-made pools. Underground tourist facilities can also needlessly pollute caves. Journeys into places like Carlsbad Cavern used to be an all-day affair. Lunch areas were created where people could eat and refresh themselves before heading on. Today, these underground lunch rooms do more than that: they have become concession areas filled with trinkets that could just as easily be sold above ground. These expanded underground tourist facilities have destroyed vast areas of caves that should have been preserved for their beauty. As visitors to caves, we need to understand that, as with most natural resources, a cave's best use is its own use.

WATER

The Source of Water

This brings us to the second meaning of "caving softly," one that is even more important than maintaining a cave's beauty. Caves are an indispensable part of the aquifers (our natural water reservoirs) found in karst (cave country). Caves often lie just above the underground water level, known as the water table. These underground aquifers are where we get most of our drinking water. We don't always connect caves with water, but caves are our windows into the water table and they must be preserved to protect our water source.

If we build sewage pits next to sinkholes, for example, and a big rain or flood hits, the sewage pit can overflow right into a sinkhole, contaminating the water for downstream towns. Aquifers are like big bathtubs: the more harmful chemicals we pour into them, the more they collect. If we are to continue to live on top of these precious water sources, we need to protect them from pollution.

Caves are places of great beauty and we need to reduce our impact on them. We have said, "Take nothing but pictures, kill nothing but time, and leave nothing behind, not even footprints." By following this motto, we make sure the next person to visit the cave will have as wonderful an experience as we had. We also have to be aware of the larger role caves play in our lives. We need to understand that caring for the environment should be a basic part of life for all people on Earth. Perhaps we should replace the notion of Mother Earth, as my four-year-old daughter suggested, with the name Family Earth, because life on this planet is all of our responsibility, not just our mother's. Besides, this Mother isn't here to pick up after us.

Maintaining unspoiled caves isn't only to please those who play in them. Unpolluted caves are important to all of us who draw fresh water from them. We must all learn to cave softly, because the cave we destroy may be the one we depend on for life.

Pollution can seep through caves into our aquifers

Caves of the National Parks

Caves in our National Park System can be found all across the country. In New England, the South, the Midwest, the Southwest, the Pacific Northwest, and the West, our national parks are filled with caves that can be explored by curious cavers. Many of these parks offer guided and self-guided tours that educate visitors about the importance and formation of these magnificent natural resources. Here is a list of some of those parks and their caves.

Arcadia National Park, Maine
Carlsbad Caverns National Park, New Mexico
Craters of the Moon National Monument, Idaho
Great Basin National Park, Nevada
Jewel Cave National Monument, South Dakota
Lava Beds National Monument, California
Mammoth Cave National Park, Kentucky
Oregon Caves National Monument, Oregon
Ozark Scenic Rivers, Missouri
Russell Cave National Monument, Alabama
Sequoia and Kings Canyon National Parks, California
Timpanogos Cave National Monument, Utah
Wind Cave National Park, South Dakota

The Guardian of the Shield in the Cave of the Madonna, New Mexico

David Jagnow

Photo facing page, Howard Crew

The Christmas Tree in Slaughter Canyon Cave, New Mexico

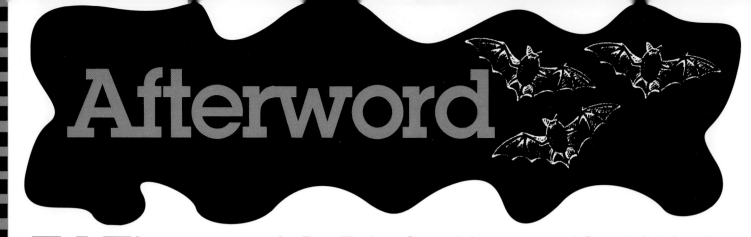

Afterword

When someone asks Ron Kerbo, Cave Management Specialist for the National Park Service, if he's ever been to the end of a cave, he smiles. From all accounts, caves don't have ends! Their passage-ways split off in all directions: up, down, side to side, forward, and back. So where is the end of the cave? Kerbo's answer is that the real end of a cave is its entrance. Cavers start their journey at a cave's end and are really looking for its beginning.

Kerbo's father never understood why his son would risk his life to venture into such dangerous and uncharted places. The only rea-son he could come up with was that his son was searching for trea-sure. Why *does* Kerbo do it? "Investigating science excites the imag-ination," he says, "and caves certainly do that. So, I guess, in some ways, my father was right. The treasures for me are the opportunity for scientific investigation, the physical challenge, and the beauty."

Yes, there are remarkable treasures to be found in caves, but they are not the kind of riches we can physically carry out with us. They are the richness of the earth's wonders, the richness of the imagination, and the richness of discovery. These are treasures we can hold inside forever. That's why it is so important to respect and protect these earthly treasures. Unlike money, they can never be replaced.

A caver at the entrance to a cave

Ronal Kerbo

Glossarized Index

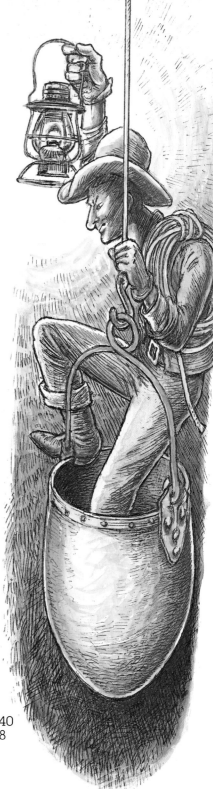

BIZARRE & BEAUTIFUL SERIES

A spirited and fun investigation of the mysteries of the five senses in the animal kingdom.

Each title is 8¹/₂" x 11", 48 pages, $14.95 hardcover, with color photographs and illustrations throughout.

Bizarre & Beautiful Ears
Bizarre & Beautiful Eyes
Bizarre & Beautiful Feelers
Bizarre & Beautiful Noses
Bizarre & Beautiful Tongues

RAINBOW WARRIOR ARTISTS SERIES

W hat is a Rainbow Warrior Artist? It is a person who strives to live in harmony with the Earth and all living creatures, and who tries to better the world while living his or her life in a creative way.

Each title is written by Reavis Moore with a foreword by LeVar Burton, and is 8¹/₂" x 11", 48 pages, $14.95 hardcover, with color photographs and illustrations.

Native Artists of Africa (available 1/94)
Native Artists of North America

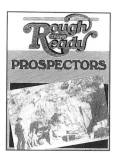

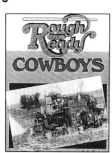

ROUGH AND READY SERIES

L earn about the men and women who settled the American frontier. Explore the myths and legends about these courageous individuals and learn about the environmental, cultural, and economic legacies they left to us.

Each title is written by A. S. Gintzler and is 48 pages, 8¹/₂" x 11", $12.95 hardcover, with two-color illustrations and duotone archival photographs.

Rough and Ready Cowboys (available 4/94)
Rough and Ready Homesteaders (available 4/94)
Rough and Ready Prospectors (available 4/94)

AMERICAN ORIGINS SERIES

M any of us are the third and fourth generation of our families to live in America. Learn what our great-great grandparents experienced when they arrived here and how much of our lives are still intertwined with theirs.

Each title is 48 pages, 8¹/₂" x 11", $12.95 hardcover, with two-color illustrations and duotone archival photographs.

Tracing Our German Roots, Leda Silver
Tracing Our Irish Roots, Sharon Moscinski
Tracing Our Italian Roots, Kathleen Lee
Tracing Our Jewish Roots, Miriam Sagan

EXTREMELY WEIRD SERIES

All of the titles are written by Sarah Lovett, 8½" x 11", 48 pages, $9.95 paperbacks, with color photographs and illustrations.

Extremely Weird Bats
Extremely Weird Birds
Extremely Weird Endangered Species
Extremely Weird Fishes
Extremely Weird Frogs
Extremely Weird Insects
Extremely Weird Mammals
Extremely Weird Micro Monsters
Extremely Weird Primates
Extremely Weird Reptiles
Extremely Weird Sea Creatures
Extremely Weird Snakes
Extremely Weird Spiders

X-RAY VISION SERIES

Each title in the series is 8½" x 11", 48 pages, $9.95 paperback, with color photographs and illustrations and written by Ron Schultz.

Looking Inside the Brain
Looking Inside Cartoon Animation
Looking Inside Caves and Caverns
Looking Inside Sports Aerodynamics
Looking Inside Sunken Treasure
Looking Inside Telescopes and the Night Sky

THE KIDDING AROUND TRAVEL GUIDES

All of the titles listed below are 64 pages and $9.95 paperbacks, except for Kidding Around the National Parks and Kidding Around Spain, which are 108 pages and $12.95 paperbacks.

Kidding Around Atlanta
Kidding Around Boston, 2nd ed.
Kidding Around Chicago, 2nd ed.
Kidding Around the Hawaiian Islands
Kidding Around London
Kidding Around Los Angeles
Kidding Around the National Parks
  of the Southwest
Kidding Around New York City, 2nd ed.
Kidding Around Paris
Kidding Around Philadelphia
Kidding Around San Diego
Kidding Around San Francisco
Kidding Around Santa Fe
Kidding Around Seattle
Kidding Around Spain
Kidding Around Washington, D.C., 2nd ed.

MASTERS OF MOTION SERIES

Each title in the series is 10¼" x 9", 48 pages, $9.95 paperback, with color photographs and illustrations.

How to Drive an Indy Race Car
  David Rubel
How to Fly a 747
  Tim Paulson
How to Fly the Space Shuttle
  Russell Shorto

THE KIDS EXPLORE SERIES

Each title is written by kids for kids by the Westridge Young Writers Workshop, 7" x 9", with photographs and illustrations by the kids.

Kids Explore America's Hispanic Heritage
112 pages, $7.95 paper
Kids Explore America's African-American Heritage
128 pages, $8.95 paper
Kids Explore the Gifts of Children with Special Needs
112 pages, $8.95 paper (available 2/94)
Kids Explore America's Japanese Heritage
112 pages, $8.95 paper (available 4/94)

ENVIRONMENTAL TITLES

Habitats: Where the Wild Things Live
Randi Hacker and Jackie Kaufman
8½" x 11", 48 pages, color illustrations, $9.95 paper

The Indian Way: Learning to Communicate with Mother Earth
Gary McLain
7" x 9", 114 pages, illustrations, $9.95 paper

Rads, Ergs, and Cheeseburgers: The Kids' Guide to Energy and the Environment
Bill Yanda
7" x 9", 108 pages, two-color illustrations, $13.95 paper

The Kids' Environment Book: What's Awry and Why
Anne Pedersen
7" x 9", 192 pages, two-color illustrations, $13.95 paper